EMBARK ON A JOURNEY OF INSPIRATION WITH THE TIMELESS TALES FROM THE LIFE OF PROPHET MUHAMMAD–PERFECT FOR YOUNG HEARTS

Preface

Welcome to "Islamic Stories For Kids: Inspiring Tales from the Life of Prophet Muhammad for Young Hearts." In the pages that follow, children will embark on a captivating journey into the life of Prophet Muhammad, peace be upon him, exploring tales that are both enlightening and filled with valuable lessons.

This collection has been thoughtfully curated to present the essence of the Prophet's life in a way that resonates with young hearts. Each story is crafted to inspire, instill moral values, and foster a love for the teachings of Islam. Through these narratives, children will encounter moments of kindness, courage, and wisdom, discovering timeless lessons that are as relevant today as they were in the Prophet's time.

As young readers delve into these stories, we hope they find joy in learning about the exemplary life of Prophet Muhammad and gain a deeper understanding of the principles that form the foundation of Islam. May this book serve as a source of inspiration, fostering a love for storytelling, learning, and, most importantly, the beautiful teachings of our beloved Prophet.

Happy reading!

Table of Content

1. The Birth of Prophet Muhammad: A Mercy to the Worlds

In the lively city of Mecca, there resided a couple named Amina and Abdullah, renowned for their benevolence, generosity, and unwavering faith in Allah. Amina, an expectant mother, eagerly anticipated the arrival of their first child.

On a serene night, with the moon casting a gentle glow, Amina had a dream where her home was filled with radiant light, surrounded by angels offering words of comfort and joy. Awaking with a profound sense of peace, she sensed a divine presence.

As time passed, the destined day arrived when Amina gave birth to a special child. Muhammad, as he was named, emerged into the world amid a gentle breeze and sweet melodies. His destiny was to be a mercy to the worlds.

Muhammad's early years were marked by kindness and compassion. His honesty, generosity, and love for all living beings made him a beacon of purity, attracting animals in Mecca to gather around him.

During his childhood, Muhammad accompanied his grandfather, Abdul-Muttalib, to the Kaaba. Witnessing the sacred structure in need of repair, he recognized the importance of unity. Rallying the people of Mecca, they collaboratively rebuilt the Kaaba, symbolizing unity and faith.

As Muhammad entered his youth, his wisdom and integrity earned him the title "Al-Amin," the trustworthy. Mecca's residents respected him deeply. When a conflict arose over the placement of the Black Stone in the reconstructed Kaaba, Muhammad, despite his youth, mediated the dispute. Placing the Black Stone on a cloth, representatives from each tribe lifted it together, resolving the matter peacefully.

Prophet Muhammad's birth heralded a new era characterized by love, compassion, and justice. His life became a source of guidance and inspiration for people of diverse backgrounds. Unbeknownst to the people of Mecca, the child born to Amina and Abdullah would grow up to be a mercy to the worlds, spreading peace and love across generations.

2. The Orphan's Journey to Leadership

In the vibrant city of Mecca, a young boy named Muhammad lived, marked by the tragedy of being an orphan. His father had passed away before his birth, and his mother left this world when he was a mere six years old.

Despite the hardships, Muhammad stood out as a special child, radiating kindness and a resilient spirit. Raised by his grandfather Abdul-Muttalib until his demise, Muhammad then found a guardian in his uncle, Abu Talib.

As he matured, Muhammad gained renown for his honesty and trustworthiness, earning the moniker "Al-Amin" from his fellow Meccans. A wealthy and noble woman named Khadijah, impressed by his character, entrusted him with managing her trade caravan. This connection blossomed into marriage, forming a loving family.

One night, while meditating in the Cave of Hira, Muhammad experienced a profound event. The angel Gabriel delivered a message from Allah, setting the stage for a new chapter in his life—the divine revelations that would later compose the Quran.

Facing opposition in Mecca as he shared these revelations, Muhammad persevered, spreading a message of peace, compassion, and the oneness of God. His leadership qualities shone brightly during the Battle of Badr, where, though outnumbered, he led with wisdom and courage to secure a decisive victory.

Throughout challenges, Muhammad's compassion remained steadfast. He forgave those who wronged him and imparted the significance of kindness and forgiveness to his followers.

As the years unfolded, the orphaned boy of Mecca transformed into Prophet Muhammad, a beloved leader cherished not only by family and friends but by all embracing the Islamic message. Grounded in justice, mercy, and a profound love for humanity, his leadership became an enduring example.

The story of this orphan's journey serves as an inspiration to people of all ages, demonstrating that with kindness, perseverance, and faith, anyone can ascend to leadership, leaving a positive impact on the world.

3. A Genuine Bond: Prophet Muhammad and Abu Bakr's Friendship

In the lively city of Mecca, dwelled Abu Bakr, a man known for his honesty, generosity, and steadfast friendship. In the same city, the esteemed Prophet Muhammad, characterized by wisdom and compassion, shared messages of love and peace one day as the sun painted the sky with warm hues.

Among the attentive crowd was Abu Bakr, deeply moved by the Prophet's words. Recognizing the truth, he hurried to the Prophet and declared his belief in Allah and the divine message. Touched by Abu Bakr's sincerity, the Prophet warmly embraced him, sealing a bond of inseparable friendship.

As Islam faced challenges in its early days, Abu Bakr remained an unwavering friend, supporting the Prophet in spreading the message despite opposition from the powerful Quraysh tribe in Mecca.

When the divine command came for the Prophet to migrate to Yathrib (later Medina), known as the Hijra, Abu Bakr selflessly offered his wealth for the journey, exemplifying true friendship and sacrifice. Together, they faced challenges on this transformative journey.

In Medina, the friendship between Prophet Muhammad and Abu Bakr deepened. Abu Bakr continued his unwavering support, contributing to the establishment of a just and compassionate community.

Their friendship's story teaches invaluable lessons on true friendship, loyalty, and selflessness. Abu Bakr's steadfast support earned him the title "Al-Siddiq," meaning "The Truthful," a reflection of his sincere belief in the Prophet's message.

The enduring legacy of their friendship inspires generations, emphasizing the importance of being true friends and selflessly supporting one another. Children, too, can draw inspiration from this tale, learning the virtues of genuine friendship exemplified by Abu Bakr towards Prophet Muhammad.

4. The Trustworthy: Young Muhammad and the Covenant of the Quraish

In the vibrant city of Mecca, resided a young boy named Muhammad, acclaimed for his honesty and integrity, earning him the endearing title "Al-Amin," meaning the Trustworthy.

Growing up amidst Mecca's bustling trade and lively marketplaces, Muhammad's uncle, Abu Talib, decided to take him on a journey to Yathrib, a city celebrated for its fertile lands. Throughout the caravan's trek across vast deserts, Muhammad observed the diverse tribes encountered, reaching Yathrib, a city grappling with internal strife.

The leaders of Yathrib, seeking a resolution, heard of Muhammad's reputation and invited him to mediate a pact fostering peace and cooperation among the tribes. Despite his youth, Muhammad exuded a grace and wisdom beyond his years, leaving the leaders eager to meet this young mediator.

Attentively listening to the leaders' challenges, Muhammad proposed the groundbreaking Pact of the Quraish. The agreement called for all Yathrib tribes, irrespective of their backgrounds, to unite as one community. Emphasizing justice, mutual protection, and the collective welfare of the city, Muhammad's proposal aimed to instill unity, compassion, and mutual respect.

Inspired by the Trustworthy's wisdom, the leaders embraced the pact. The Pact of the Quraish heralded a new era for Yathrib, renamed Medina, meaning "the City of the Prophet." The city thrived with cooperation, mutual support, and harmony.

Upon returning to Mecca, Muhammad's reputation as the Trustworthy continued to soar. Unbeknownst to the people of Mecca, this young boy would eventually become Prophet Muhammad, the Messenger of Allah, guiding a community founded on principles of justice, compassion, and unity.

The tale of the Trustworthy, Young Muhammad, and the Covenant of the Quraish became an enduring source of inspiration, imparting lessons of trust, unity, and collaborative efforts for the greater good to generations to come.

5. The Sacred Cave: Revelation of the Quran

In the bustling city of Mecca, there lived a humble and kind-hearted man named Muhammad, renowned for his honesty, generosity, and love for those around him. His reputation as Al-Amin, the trustworthy, reflected the deep respect people had for him.

Seeking solitude for reflection, Muhammad climbed the rocky hills surrounding Mecca one day and discovered a secluded cave known as Hira. This unassuming cave would become the sacred space where a momentous event unfolded.

Under the gentle glow of the moon, Muhammad entered the tranquil cave to contemplate the beauty of the universe, the Creator, and the purpose of life. Little did he know that this night would mark a profound turning point in his life.

During a peaceful night of deep contemplation and prayer, the angel Jibreel descended from the heavens with a message from Allah. The cave was bathed in divine light as Jibreel spoke, "Read, in the name of your Lord who created."

Surprised and awestruck, Muhammad replied, "I am not learned. What shall I read?" The angel insisted, encouraging Muhammad to repeat verses after him. In that blessed cave, the first verses of the Quran were revealed to Prophet Muhammad.

The profound words, filled with wisdom, guided humanity to worship the One true God, practice justice and kindness, and care for one another. Embracing this divine message, Muhammad became the Prophet, realizing he was chosen to be a messenger to his people.

Over the years, more revelations continued to be sent down, offering guidance, comfort, and solutions to challenges faced by the community. The Quran became a source of light and hope, transforming the lives of its followers.

The cave of Hira remained a sacred place, a reminder of the night when the heavens opened, and God's words were revealed. Pilgrims and believers, young and old, visited the cave, sensing the presence of the divine and the love that altered the course of history.

The story of the Cave of Hira and the revelation of the Quran teaches the power of reflection, prayer, and the profound impact of divine guidance on Prophet Muhammad's life. It is a tale of spiritual discovery that continues to inspire people worldwide to seek wisdom and goodness in their own lives.

6. Prophet Muhammad and Abu Bakr: The Shelter of Thawr Cave

In the vast deserts of Arabia, a noble and trustworthy man named Abu Bakr shared an unbreakable bond with the beloved Prophet Muhammad (peace be upon him). Their friendship, rooted in faith and love for Allah, stood resilient against the trials they faced.

One day, at sunset, the Prophet Muhammad received a divine message instructing him to leave Mecca for the awaiting believers in Medina. Aware of the challenges ahead, especially from the leaders of Mecca, who opposed his message, the Prophet, accompanied by Abu Bakr, embarked on a clandestine journey to Medina.

The moonlit path was fraught with challenges, with pursuers close behind, driven by malice. Yet, the unwavering bond of friendship and shared faith between the Prophet and Abu Bakr fortified their determination.

Journeying through the desert, they sought refuge in Thawr Cave. In the cave's darkness, the true test of their friendship unfolded. Concerned for the Prophet's safety, Abu Bakr proposed blocking the cave entrance with his own body to ensure his friend's protection.

Touched by Abu Bakr's selfless offer, the Prophet, with gratitude, suggested trusting in Allah and relying on His protection. This moment showcased the deep faith and trust both men placed in their Creator.

As the pursuers neared the cave, they found it seemingly untouched, sealed by a delicate web spun by a spider and guarded by a nesting dove. Convinced that no one could be inside, they passed by, unaware of the hidden travelers.

The journey continued, and the friends reached Medina safely, welcomed by its people. The city became a sanctuary for the growing Muslim community.

The story of Thawr Cave teaches us the power of friendship, faith, and trust in Allah. It underscores that even in the face of challenges, true friends stand steadfast, and Allah's protection is ever-present for those who place their trust in Him. The enduring friendship between Prophet Muhammad and Abu Bakr serves as a timeless example for generations, highlighting the strength found in true companionship and unwavering trust in divine guidance.

7. The Prophet's Compassion: A Lesson from the Hurting Camel

In the city of Medina, during the time of Prophet Muhammad, peace be upon him, there resided a man who owned a mistreated camel.

Known for overloading the camel with heavy burdens and displaying little concern for its well-being, the owner's actions caught the attention of the Prophet as he passed by.

Approaching the owner with gentleness, the Prophet reminded him of the responsibility humans bear towards animals. He stressed that animals, as creations of Allah, should be treated with kindness and compassion.

Seeing the distress of the camel, the Prophet took swift action. Speaking to the owner with wisdom and empathy, he conveyed that every living being, including animals, possesses rights and deserves fair treatment. The impact of the Prophet's words prompted immediate remorse from the owner.

Demonstrating unparalleled compassion, the Prophet tenderly touched the hurting camel, alleviating its pain. Remarkably, the camel, seemingly understanding the kindness shown, responded positively to the Prophet's touch.

Addressing the people of Medina, the Prophet delivered a profound message on the importance of showing mercy towards animals. He emphasized that the moral character of humanity is reflected even in the treatment of animals.

This incident stands as a well-documented example of the Prophet's teachings on compassion towards animals, recorded in various hadith collections, including those by Imam Bukhari and Imam Muslim. It underscores the significance of treating animals with care and respect.

The story of the Prophet and the hurting camel remains a timeless lesson, urging Muslims to follow his example of compassion towards all of Allah's creations and cultivating a culture of empathy and kindness.

8. The Prophet's Kindness: Zaynab's Misplaced Necklace

In the heart of Medina, a cheerful young girl named Zaynab was known for her infectious smile and compassionate spirit. One day, while playing near the Prophet's Mosque, she realized her cherished necklace, a gift from her beloved mother, was missing.

Distressed and on the verge of tears, Zaynab began searching every corner of the mosque and its surroundings. Unbeknownst to her, the Prophet Muhammad (peace be upon him) observed her distress from a distance.

Approaching Zaynab with a comforting smile, the Prophet inquired, "What troubles you, my dear?"

Holding back tears, Zaynab explained her predicament, describing the lost necklace, a gift from her dearly loved mother.

With a heart full of compassion, the Prophet assured her, "Do not worry, Zaynab. We will find your necklace, Insha'Allah."

Summoning some companions who were present, the Prophet organized a search for the misplaced necklace. They meticulously combed through the mosque, the nearby market, and the streets of Medina. The Prophet actively joined the search, emphasizing the importance of aiding those in need.

After a thorough exploration, the necklace was discovered in a corner of the mosque. Delighted with the find, the companions returned it to Zaynab.

Overwhelmed with joy, Zaynab exclaimed, "Thank you, Messenger of Allah! Your heart is so kind and caring."

The Prophet smiled and replied, "In helping one another, we find joy. Your happiness is dear to me, and it is our duty to assist those facing difficulties. Never hesitate to seek help when needed."

This documented incident became a cherished memory in Medina, illustrating the Prophet's compassion not only for adults but also for the youngest members of the community. Zaynab's lost necklace serves as a lesson for generations, highlighting the importance of compassion, community support, and the Prophet's unwavering care for every individual, regardless of age.

9. The Miraculous Night Journey: A Divine Blessing

In the vibrant city of Mecca, a man named Muhammad resided, destined to become the Prophet of Islam. One night, a celestial event unfolded, altering his life and the course of Islamic history.

Under the moonlit sky, with stars shimmering brightly, Prophet Muhammad (peace be upon him) rested near the Kaaba. In this serene moment, the angel Jibreel (Gabriel) descended from the heavens, bearing a special gift from Allah.

"Prophet Muhammad," announced Jibreel, "Allah has chosen you for an extraordinary journey tonight. Prepare yourself, for this will be a unique and unparalleled experience."

Guided by Jibreel, the Prophet was led to Buraq, a magnificent creature with wings that sparkled like the night sky. In an instant, he found himself riding this celestial being.

They traversed the vast darkness, arriving at the sacred city of Jerusalem. Here, the Prophet stood in the revered Al-Aqsa Mosque, joining the assembly of prophets, including Moses and Jesus (peace be upon them).

A celestial ladder appeared, and the Prophet ascended through the heavens, passing through seven levels. At each stage, he encountered revered prophets such as Adam, Noah, and Ibrahim (peace be upon them), who greeted him warmly with words of encouragement.

Reaching the highest point, Sidrat al-Muntaha, a tree of unparalleled beauty, the Prophet received divine commandments on prayer and fundamental aspects of Islamic teachings directly from Allah.

After this enlightening experience, the Prophet descended back to Jerusalem and then returned to Mecca, all within the blink of an eye. As he lay near the Kaaba, he reflected on the miraculous journey that had unfolded.

The Night Journey was a divine gift, affirming the Prophet's unique role in Allah's plan. It emphasized the significance of prayer, unity among prophets, and the profound connection between the earthly and heavenly realms.
Children, whenever you gaze at the moonlit sky, recall the extraordinary journey of Prophet Muhammad (peace be upon him) and the divine messages that illuminate our lives.

10. The Prophet and the Benevolent Companion: Abu Talha's Orchard

In the lively city of Medina, a devoted companion of Prophet Muhammad (peace be upon him), named Abu Talha, was recognized for his wealth and the flourishing orchards he owned. One particular orchard, known as Bairuha, held significant sentimental value to him.

When the Prophet learned of Abu Talha's deep connection to this orchard, he approached him with a request. "Abu Talha, would you consider donating the orchard of Bairuha for the sake of Allah? The rewards in the Hereafter would be immense," the Prophet suggested.

Initially surprised by the request and attached to his orchard, Abu Talha, a man of profound faith and generosity, contemplated the opportunity to please Allah. Acknowledging the Prophet's guidance, he graciously agreed to part with the orchard.

In a spirit of selflessness, Abu Talha informed the Prophet, saying, "O Messenger of Allah, I give away Bairuha in the cause of Allah, just as you have advised."

Expressing his gratitude, the Prophet Muhammad, with a radiant smile, prayed, "May Allah bless your wealth and family, Abu Talha."

Abu Talha's charitable act did not end with the donation. He generously distributed the orchard's produce among the needy, ensuring that the blessings reached the entire community. His exemplary generosity inspired others to follow suit, fostering a culture of benevolence in Medina.

This incident is documented in various hadith collections, including Sahih Bukhari and Sahih Muslim, emphasizing the Prophet's teachings on the significance of charity and selflessness. Abu Talha's sacrifice remains a timeless lesson, illustrating the Prophet's ability to guide his companions toward actions that yield both worldly and eternal rewards.

The story of Abu Talha's orchard reflects the principles of charity, sacrifice, and the Prophet's influence in inspiring positive change in the hearts of his companions, contributing to the formation of a compassionate and selfless community.

11. The Constitution of Medina: A Blueprint for Harmony

In the enchanting city of Medina, diverse communities coexisted – Muslims, Jews, and others – all sharing a dream of living together in peace. To guide them in this endeavor, the wise leader was none other than Prophet Muhammad (peace be upon him), the Messenger of Allah.

Gathering the people in a large open space, the Prophet (peace be upon him) spoke warmly about unity, kindness, and justice. Emphasizing their collective identity, he proposed a transformative agreement known as the Constitution of Medina – a magical document holding the key to building a just society.

Within this constitution, the Prophet (peace be upon him) ensured that everyone, regardless of their faith, had the right to live peacefully and practice their religion freely. He fostered a sense of equality, treating the diverse community as one extended family.

The Constitution of Medina also outlined rules for conflict resolution, promoting dialogue and understanding. The Prophet (peace be upon him) encouraged the people to listen to one another, emphasizing the importance of peaceful solutions to disputes, ensuring that everyone felt heard and valued.

A remarkable aspect of the constitution was its focus on protecting the vulnerable. The Prophet (peace be upon him) ensured that orphans, widows, and those in need received special care and support from the community, reflecting the kindness and compassion taught by Islam towards the less fortunate.

As days turned into weeks, and weeks into months, the people of Medina worked collaboratively to construct a society grounded in justice and fairness. Laughter echoed through the streets, and the air carried the sweet scent of unity.

The Constitution of Medina became a guiding beacon for future generations, showcasing how diverse communities could harmoniously coexist. Under the wise leadership of Prophet Muhammad (peace be upon him), the people of Medina demonstrated that when different hearts unite, they can create a society that is just, caring, and truly enchanting. Thus, the city of Medina thrived as a shining example of love and cooperation for all.

12. The Prophet's Guidance: The Upright Merchant

In the bustling marketplace of Medina, a merchant named Ali distinguished himself for his unwavering honesty and integrity in all his transactions.

One day, faced with a moral dilemma, Ali discovered a bag of gold coins that a customer had mistakenly left behind. Choosing the path of righteousness, Ali decided to seek guidance from the wise Prophet Muhammad (peace be upon him). With the bag of gold in hand, he approached the Prophet, greeted him respectfully, and explained the situation.

Recognizing Ali's sincerity, the Prophet commended him for his honesty. He gathered the people in the marketplace and shared Ali's story as an exemplar of integrity and righteousness.

"O people of Medina," the Prophet addressed the crowd, "Ali has demonstrated the true essence of honesty. Even when tempted by unexpected wealth, he chose the path of righteousness."

The assembled crowd listened attentively as the Prophet continued, "In Islam, honesty extends beyond mere words; it encompasses truthful actions. Ali's conduct today exemplifies the values that fortify our community, making it strong and just."

Turning to Ali, the Prophet stated, "Your honesty will be rewarded in both this world and the Hereafter. Continue being a beacon of integrity for your fellow citizens."

The news of Ali's honesty spread throughout Medina, establishing him as a respected figure known for his principled behavior. Merchants and customers sought his services, confident in the implicit trust they could place in him.

This documented incident, found in various historical accounts, serves as a timeless lesson emphasizing the importance of honesty and integrity in daily life. It underscores the Prophet's role as a guide and exemplar, reinforcing the values essential for a just and virtuous society. The story of Ali, the upright merchant, remains an enduring source of inspiration, encouraging individuals to uphold the principles of honesty and righteousness in their interactions with others.

13. The Prophet's Grandsons and the Extended Prayer

During one of the Prophet Muhammad's prayers at the mosque in Medina, his two young grandsons, Hasan and Husayn, who were still very small, entered the prayer area. Upon noticing them, the Prophet greeted them with a warm smile and continued with his prayer.

As the Prophet went into prostration, he extended the duration of this position, which was unusual. The companions, observing this, were intrigued by the extended prostration. Once the prayer concluded, some of them inquired about the reason behind the prolonged posture.

With kindness and a smile, the Prophet explained, "While I was in prayer, Hasan and Husayn climbed onto my back. Not wishing to disturb their playful innocence, I chose to prolong my prostration until they voluntarily climbed off."

This heartwarming incident beautifully exemplifies the Prophet's deep compassion and his priority to ensure the comfort and well-being of children, even during the sacred moments of his prayer. The story, documented in various hadith collections, including Sahih al-Bukhari and Sahih Muslim, serves as a touching reminder of the Prophet's love for children and his consideration for their needs, even in the midst of his devotion.

14. The Prophet's Forgiveness: The Conquest of Mecca

In the ancient city of Mecca, a significant moment unfolded as Prophet Muhammad, peace be upon him, approached the city with a large Muslim army, signaling the conquest of Mecca. Despite years of opposition and persecution from the people of Mecca, the Prophet's response was not one of revenge but rather marked by compassion and forgiveness.

As the Muslim forces entered Mecca, they did so with humility. Riding on his camel, the Prophet entered the city with his head bowed in gratitude to Allah. This display of unexpected humility left the people of Mecca astonished.

Making his way to the Kaaba, the sacred house of worship, the Prophet stood near it while the people of Mecca awaited their fate, anticipating possible retribution for past conflicts. However, the Prophet's actions took a different turn.

In a remarkable moment, the Prophet, with tears in his eyes, raised his hands and prayed for forgiveness. He spoke words of mercy and love, echoing the Quranic verse: "No reproach this day shall be on you; Allah will forgive you, and He is the Most Merciful of the merciful."

This unexpected act of forgiveness profoundly impacted the people of Mecca. Witnessing the Prophet's magnanimity, many embraced Islam willingly, not out of fear but out of admiration for the Prophet's capacity for mercy.

The conquest of Mecca thus became a triumph of mercy over vengeance and love over hatred. The Prophet Muhammad, peace be upon him, forgave even those who had been staunch enemies, showcasing the true essence of forgiveness and compassion.

This historic event is well-documented in various Islamic sources, including the Quran and authentic hadith collections such as Sahih al-Bukhari and Sahih Muslim. It stands as a powerful example of the Prophet's unwavering commitment to forgiveness and his ability to transform adversaries into allies through the force of compassion.

15. The Prophet's Garden: An Oasis of Environmental Stewardship

In the bustling city of Medina, nestled in the heart of the Arabian Peninsula, the Prophet Muhammad, peace be upon him, demonstrated not only spiritual leadership but also a deep commitment to environmental stewardship. His actions and teachings emphasized the importance of caring for the Earth and all its creatures.

One day, as the sun cast its golden glow over the city, the Prophet walked through the narrow streets, surrounded by his companions. Observing a group of children playing near a well, he imparted a valuable lesson: "Water is precious. Do not waste it, even if you are by a flowing river."

Continuing his walk, the Prophet arrived at a barren piece of land on the outskirts of the city. With a twinkle in his eye, he envisioned transforming this desolate area into a lush garden—a haven for both people and wildlife.

Gathering the community, the Prophet shared his vision, and inspired by his words, his companions eagerly joined hands to cultivate the land. Date palms, fruit-bearing trees, and fragrant flowers were planted, turning the once-barren space into a thriving oasis.

As the garden flourished, the Prophet established guidelines for its care, emphasizing the importance of conserving water, avoiding waste, and treating animals with kindness. The garden became a model of sustainable living, reflecting the Prophet's commitment to environmental harmony.

One day, a companion named Abu Talha admired the garden and decided to donate his nearby orchard, filled with lush date palms, to the community for the greater good. The Prophet accepted the generous gift and proposed using the orchard's proceeds to support the less fortunate in Medina. This act of charity, combined with sustainable practices, created a harmonious balance between environmental conservation and social welfare.

The Prophet's garden in Medina serves as a timeless symbol of his teachings on environmental stewardship. It reminds people of all ages that taking care of the Earth is a noble responsibility—one that reflects the values of Islam and the wisdom of Prophet Muhammad, the Mercy to the Worlds.

16. The Prophet's Wisdom: The Treaty of Hudaybiyyah

In the year 628 CE, the Prophet Muhammad, peace be upon him, embarked on a journey from Medina with a group of companions to perform the pilgrimage in Mecca. This journey led to the Treaty of Hudaybiyyah, a pivotal moment in Islamic history.

Approaching Mecca, the Quraysh, reluctant to allow the Muslims to perform the pilgrimage, intercepted them at Hudaybiyyah. Despite the Prophet's peaceful intentions, tensions rose, and it seemed the pilgrimage might not occur.

Guided by divine wisdom, the Prophet engaged in negotiations with the Quraysh leaders. After much discussion, a treaty was drafted. However, the terms were not entirely favorable to the Muslims, leading to disappointment among some companions who couldn't understand why seemingly unfair conditions had to be accepted.

One condition stated that the Muslims would return to Medina without performing the pilgrimage that year. Despite initial discontent, the Prophet's wisdom shone through as he recognized the strategic importance of accepting these terms for the greater good.

In the days that followed, an incident highlighted the profound wisdom behind the Prophet's decision. A group of Muslims was sent to negotiate with the Quraysh on behalf of their brethren. One of the Quraysh leaders, Urwah ibn Mas'ud, was amazed by the level of respect and loyalty the Muslims showed to the Prophet.

Upon returning to the Quraysh leaders, Urwah said, "I have visited the courts of Caesar, Khosrow, and Negus, but never have I seen a king so revered by his people as Muhammad is by his companions. They would not allow even a drop of rain to fall on him without collecting it and rubbing it on their faces. If he spat, it would not fall except in the hand of one of them who would rub it on his face and skin."

This unwavering loyalty and love for the Prophet left a lasting impression on the Quraysh leaders, softening their hearts towards the Muslims and Islam.

The Treaty of Hudaybiyyah, initially challenging for the Muslims, turned out to be a strategic move that paved the way for a period of peace and increased acceptance of Islam in the Arabian Peninsula. The wisdom of the Prophet Muhammad, peace be upon him, played a crucial role in laying the groundwork for the eventual conquest of Mecca and the spread of Islam across the region.

17. The Battle of Uhud: Endurance Amidst Trials

In the annals of Islamic history, the Battle of Uhud stands as a testament to the unwavering courage and resilience displayed by Prophet Muhammad, peace be upon him, and his devoted followers.

On a radiant day, the Muslim community, led by the Prophet himself, embarked on a significant encounter with the Quraysh in the valley of Uhud. Initially met with success, a pivotal moment occurred when a misunderstanding of the Prophet's orders led a group to deviate from their assigned position on the battlefield. This deviation marked a turning point, and the tides of the battle shifted against the Muslims.

Prophet Muhammad, amidst the chaos, bore the brunt of adversity. Despite enduring injuries and hardship, his patience and determination remained unshaken. The sorrow deepened as news arrived of the martyrdom of the Prophet's beloved uncle, Hamza, a revered companion.

Surveying the challenging landscape, the Prophet gathered his companions, imparting a crucial lesson on the significance of patience in the face of adversity. He urged them not to despair but to place their trust in the divine plan of Allah.

Amidst the wounded, a young companion named Abdullah ibn Jubair approached the Prophet with tears in his eyes, seeking assurance about his place in Paradise. Recognizing the sincerity and courage within the young man, the Prophet affirmed, "Yes, you will enter Paradise."

The Battle of Uhud left an indelible mark on the Muslim community, teaching a profound lesson in patience. It underscored that success and victory may not always be immediate; sometimes, hardships serve as a test of faith and perseverance.

The enduring patience of Prophet Muhammad during adversity became a guiding light for generations. The lessons drawn from Uhud inspired the Muslim community to face trials with resilience, trusting in Allah's wisdom. True victory, they learned, lies in remaining steadfast on the path of righteousness.

The Battle of Uhud remains etched in Islamic history, serving as a poignant reminder of the importance of patience and unwavering trust in Allah during the most challenging times.

18. The Prophet and the Jewish Neighbor: A Lesson in Mutual Respect

In the early days of Islam, within the city of Medina, resided a Jewish man named Zayd. Renowned for his wisdom, kindness, and deep reverence for his own religious beliefs, Zayd's dwelling was situated in close proximity to that of Prophet Muhammad, peace be upon him. Their paths frequently intersected in the ordinary course of daily life.

One day, as the Prophet strolled through the neighborhood, he noticed a change in Zayd's demeanor, indicating that he was unwell. Driven by genuine concern for his neighbor's health, the Prophet approached Zayd and inquired, "How are you feeling, my friend?"

Although taken aback by the sincere care demonstrated by the Prophet, Zayd warmly responded, "I appreciate your concern, O Muhammad. Today, I am not feeling well."

Exemplifying his compassionate nature, the Prophet extended his assistance, "Is there anything I can do for you? Perhaps bring you some food or water?"

Touched by the Prophet's benevolence, Zayd expressed his gratitude, saying, "Thank you, Muhammad. Your offer alone has lifted my spirits. I will be fine, but your concern means a great deal to me."

As time elapsed, the Prophet and Zayd continued their interactions marked by mutual respect and kindness. They exchanged greetings, inquired about each other's well-being, and shared moments of laughter. Zayd admired the Prophet's commitment to fostering a peaceful and harmonious community in Medina.

On a different occasion, while the Prophet sat with his companions, a funeral procession passed by. Out of respect for the departed soul, the Prophet stood up. One of his companions remarked, "This is the funeral of a Jew, O Messenger of Allah!"

Responding with profound wisdom that mirrored his principles of justice and respect for all humanity, the Prophet stated, "Is it not a soul?"

The Prophet's words underscored the sanctity of human life, transcending religious or ethnic affiliations, and underscored his unwavering dedication to treating everyone with kindness and fairness.

This authentic account from Islamic history, documented in various hadith collections, serves as a compelling illustration of the Prophet's teachings on mutual respect, kindness, and consideration for neighbors, irrespective of their religious background. It vividly portrays the Islamic principles of compassion, understanding, and the construction of robust and harmonious communities.

19. The Prophet's Modesty: A Lesson in Humility

In the ancient city of Mecca, there resided a man named Muhammad, peace be upon him, who was not merely a leader but the final Prophet chosen by Allah to guide the people. His life served as a radiant model of humility and modesty.

On a certain day, a man from a distant tribe arrived in Mecca, drawn by the tales of the Prophet's wisdom and seeking to meet him. Unfamiliar with the faces of the locals, he found it challenging to identify the Prophet amidst the crowd.

Unlike other leaders who adorned thrones, the Prophet, peace be upon him, often sat on the ground, surrounded by his companions. Observing the visitor's perplexity, the Prophet approached him quietly, introducing himself, "Peace be upon you. I am Muhammad, the Messenger of Allah. How may I help you?"

Surprised and humbled by the Prophet's modesty, the visitor replied, "I came to learn from you. They say you are a wise and humble leader."

With a warm smile, the Prophet invited the man to sit with him. Instead of selecting a distinguished spot, he humbly chose a place on the ground, urging the visitor to join him.

As they sat together, the Prophet shared insights about kindness, honesty, and the significance of assisting others. The man from the distant tribe was deeply moved by the Prophet's words and the simplicity with which they were conveyed.

Before parting ways, the man questioned the Prophet, "Why do you sit on the ground like everyone else? You are a great leader; surely, you deserve a special place."

The Prophet, peace be upon him, responded, "I am a servant of Allah, and my mission is to guide and serve humanity. I wish to remain close to the people, to listen to their concerns, and to share in their joys and sorrows. Such is the path of humility and modesty."

Departing Mecca, the man carried with him a heart brimming with gratitude and a profound lesson in humility. The Prophet's modesty had etched an enduring impression, teaching all that authentic greatness resides in serving others with a humble heart.

This narrative is drawn from authentic hadiths present in various collections, including Sahih al-Bukhari and Sahih Muslim, highlighting the Prophet's humility and his approachability towards individuals from all walks of life.

20. Kindness in the Face of Mockery: The Prophet's Exemplary Response

In the vibrant streets of Mecca, during the initial days of Islam, Prophet Muhammad, peace be upon him, encountered numerous challenges while preaching the message of monotheism. Opposition came in various forms, including mockery from a group of individuals who sought to insult and deride him.

As the Prophet navigated through the market, sharing the message of peace and compassion, a gathering of mischievous youths converged around him, subjecting him to ridicule and mockery. Undeterred by their disrespectful behavior, the Prophet remained composed, steadfastly continuing his mission.

Observing this unjust treatment, a woman named Fatimah felt compelled to intervene. Rushing forward with a basket of dates, she offered the gift to the Prophet, who accepted it graciously, responding with a warm smile.

Amidst the insults, one mocker, intrigued by the Prophet's serene reaction, questioned his choice of responding with kindness. The Prophet, in his gentle manner, explained that insults could not alter the truth. His purpose was to share a message of mercy, compassion, and unity. He encouraged those willing to listen with open hearts to discover the beauty within these teachings.

This incident, documented in historical accounts, highlights the Prophet's exemplary response to adversity. His ability to counter mockery with patience and kindness serves as a profound lesson. By choosing compassion and resilience in the face of negativity, the Prophet not only won the hearts of onlookers but also paved the way for transformative change in the hearts of those who initially opposed him.

21. Family Harmony: The Prophet's Lessons in Love and Respect

In the ancient city of Medina, the Prophet Muhammad, peace be upon him, resided in a modest and welcoming home with his cherished family. Central to this family circle were his beloved daughter, Fatimah, and her husband, Ali ibn Abi Talib.

As the sun dipped below the horizon, casting a warm glow, the family gathered in the tranquil courtyard to share a simple meal and exchange stories. Known for his warmth and humility, the Prophet sat with his family, exemplifying kindness and respect in every interaction.

Observing her father closely, Fatimah noticed his attentive listening, shared responsibilities at home, and his loving consideration for each family member. Intrigued by these qualities, she approached him one evening.

"O Messenger of Allah," Fatimah inquired, "how do you consistently show such love and respect to everyone in our family?"

The Prophet, with a gentle smile, shared his wisdom, "My dear Fatimah, love and respect are the foundations of a strong family. Treat each other with kindness, listen openly, and always be ready to forgive. In doing so, you build a home filled with tranquility and joy."

Inspired by her father's teachings, Fatimah, alongside her husband Ali, dedicated themselves to creating a home that mirrored these principles.

Through the passing years, the family faced challenges and celebrated triumphs, guided by the enduring lessons of compassion and understanding. A visitor, noting the peaceful atmosphere in their home, sought the secret to their family harmony.

Fatimah, with a smile, replied, "In our home, we follow the example set by the Prophet Muhammad, peace be upon him. Love and respect are our guiding lights, and by treating each other with kindness, we build a strong and united family."

Thus, in the heart of Medina, the Prophet's family showcased timeless lessons of love and respect, leaving behind a legacy that continues to inspire families worldwide.

22. The Prophet's Integrity: Upholding Truth in the Face of Slander

In the lively city of Medina, where the Prophet Muhammad, peace be upon him, shared the teachings of Islam, a challenging incident unfolded, testing the strength of truth and the Prophet's character.

A man named Abdullah ibn Ubayy, harboring resentment towards the Prophet, spread a harmful rumor about Aisha, the beloved wife of the Prophet. The rumor caused distress among the Muslim community, creating a tense atmosphere.

Upon hearing the troubling news, the Prophet decided to address the community directly. Calm and composed, he gathered the people and spoke with unwavering determination.

"O believers," the Prophet began, "I have heard what people are saying. But know this, if my daughter Aisha is innocent, Allah will surely reveal the truth to us."

Turning to Aisha, the Prophet asked her to share her side of the story. Despite the deep hurt caused by the slander, Aisha spoke with innocence and truth, recounting the events in detail.

As Aisha spoke, the truth became unmistakable. The Prophet's face remained calm, reflecting his trust in Aisha and his commitment to justice.

During this challenging time, Quranic verses were revealed, affirming Aisha's innocence and admonishing those who spread false rumors. The revelation not only cleared Aisha's name but also imparted a profound lesson in truth, justice, and the consequences of baseless accusations.

Known for his forgiveness and mercy, the Prophet did not hold grudges against those who had spread the slander. Instead, he encouraged the community to learn from the incident, emphasizing the impact of words on others.

This true story, documented in various hadith collections, including Sahih al-Bukhari and Sahih Muslim, serves as a powerful lesson in seeking the truth, avoiding baseless accusations, and demonstrating patience and forgiveness, even in the face of adversity.

23. The Prophet's Prayer: A Divine Connection

In the ancient city of Mecca, a man named Muhammad, destined to become the beloved Prophet of Islam, lived a life deeply connected to the divine.

As the sun cast a warm glow over the sacred Kaaba, the Prophet Muhammad, peace be upon him, stood in solitary contemplation. Prepared to engage in one of the most intimate acts of worship, his prayer was more than a ritual; it was a profound conversation with Allah—a moment of deep reflection, gratitude, and submission.

Witnessing the Prophet's devotion, his companions were curious about the unique bond he shared with Allah through his prayers. A young girl named Aisha, who would later become a renowned scholar and the

Prophet's wife, asked, "O Messenger of Allah, why do you pray so much? Doesn't Allah already forgive your past and future sins?"

With a gentle smile, the Prophet replied, "Should I not be a grateful servant?" He explained that prayer wasn't merely about seeking forgiveness but maintaining an unbroken connection with Allah—a heartfelt conversation expressing gratitude for blessings and seeking guidance in every aspect of life.

As the sun dipped below the horizon, the Prophet stood on the soft desert sand, hands raised in supplication. His sincere words and devoted heart conveyed gratitude to the Creator. The companions, watching in awe, learned that prayer was not an obligation but a source of strength, solace, and closeness to Allah.

The story of the Prophet's prayer imparts a timeless lesson—to approach prayer not as a burden but as a divine gift. It is a direct line to Allah, bringing peace, guidance, and purpose to our lives, inspiring both children and adults to embrace prayer with renewed understanding and sincerity.

24. The Prophet's Garden of Love: Anas ibn Malik's Joyful Tale

In the vibrant city of Medina, young Anas ibn Malik, blessed with the privilege of serving the Prophet Muhammad, peace be upon him, encountered a heartwarming surprise.

While assisting in the Prophet's household, Anas discovered a beautiful garden adjacent to the Prophet's home, adorned with vibrant flowers and emanating a sweet fragrance. Intrigued, he approached the Prophet with curiosity.

"O Messenger of Allah, whose magnificent garden is this?" Anas inquired.

The Prophet, with a warm smile, responded, "It is yours, Anas. All these flowers are a gift for you."

Overwhelmed with joy, Anas devoted his days to tending to the blossoms, enveloped in the love and care bestowed upon him by the Prophet.

One afternoon, while engrossed in his work, Anas welcomed a group of curious children passing by. Inviting them into the garden, they shared laughter, games, and stories amid the beauty of the blossoms.

As the sun dipped below the horizon, Anas gathered the children and imparted the Prophet's teachings on love and kindness. The importance of nurturing relationships and spreading joy resonated in his words.

News of the Prophet's garden of love spread, attracting more children to join Anas in afternoons filled with laughter and shared happiness. The garden became a cherished space for learning and bonding.

In later years, Anas, now an adult, fondly recalled the Prophet's thoughtful gift and the valuable lessons learned in that enchanting garden. He continued to embody the spirit of love and generosity, passing down the Prophet's teachings to future generations.

This authentic and documented tale of Anas ibn Malik reflects the Prophet's affection for children and underscores the significance of cultivating spaces infused with kindness and joy—a legacy that continues to touch the hearts of those touched by the Prophet's boundless compassion.

25. The Battle of Badr: Triumph through Unwavering Faith

In the early chapters of Islamic history, a defining moment unfolded—the Battle of Badr. This crucial event tested the resolve and faith of the Muslim community in Medina.

Upon receiving news of a large caravan heading towards the city, Prophet Muhammad, peace be upon him, and his companions, who had recently migrated to Medina, sought a peaceful interception. However, the leaders of Mecca, determined to protect their wealth, dispatched a force to confront the Muslims, setting the stage for the Battle of Badr.

Despite being outnumbered and lacking resources, the Muslim army, inspired by the Prophet's unwavering confidence and faith in Allah, stood resolute. Among them was Ali ibn Abi Talib, a young man known for his courage and loyalty.

As the battle commenced, the odds appeared insurmountable. However, the Muslims, anchored by their unwavering faith and trust in Allah, faced the challenge with steadfast determination. Prophet Muhammad, with conviction in his heart, raised his hands in prayer, seeking divine support. His plea resonated with the essence of faith: "O Allah, if this small band of believers perishes, who will be left to worship You on Earth?"

In the midst of the Battle of Badr, unexpected turns transpired. Despite their numerical disadvantage, the Muslims witnessed divine intervention as angels descended to assist them, ultimately securing victory.

The triumph at Badr surpassed mere military success; it stood as a testament to the potency of faith, unwavering trust in Allah, and the steadfast commitment of the early Muslim community. The Battle of Badr echoes through Islamic history, delivering a powerful lesson that genuine triumph emerges from faith, resilience, and reliance on the guidance of Allah.

This narrative serves as a timeless source of inspiration, teaching generations that even in the face of seemingly insurmountable challenges, true victory is attainable through unyielding faith and trust in Allah's wisdom.

26. The Prophet and the Envious Companion: A Lesson in Overcoming Jealousy

In the era of Prophet Muhammad, peace be upon him, a companion named K'ab ibn Malik faced a challenging situation that put his faith and sincerity to the test.

K'ab, known for his prosperity, particularly a fruitful date palm grove, had a fellow Muslim neighbor harboring envy in his heart. Driven by jealousy, this neighbor began spreading false rumors about K'ab's wealth and intentions.

The rumors reached the Prophet's ears, prompting him to address the matter directly. He summoned both K'ab and his envious neighbor separately to hear their perspectives. K'ab, with sincerity, explained that his wealth was earned through lawful means, dedicated to charitable purposes and aiding those in need.

Guided by divine wisdom, the Prophet counseled the envious neighbor, advising against harboring envy and spreading falsehoods. Recognizing his error, the neighbor repented and sought forgiveness from both Allah and K'ab.

To underscore the gravity of envy and highlight the importance of repentance, the Prophet shared a profound hadith: "Beware! Envy consumes good deeds just as fire consumes dry wood. Remove envy by seeking forgiveness and purifying your heart."

Humbled by the Prophet's words, the envious neighbor actively worked to overcome jealousy, seeking forgiveness from K'ab and initiating positive change in his behavior. This transformative incident not only mended the relationship between the two companions but also served as a potent lesson on the perils of envy, the significance of repentance, and the Prophet's role as a mediator and guide in resolving conflicts within the Muslim community.

27. The Honored Guest: A Lesson in Equality from the Prophet's Table

In the vibrant streets of Medina, lived a humble man named Abdullah—a soul known for his kindness, humility, and unyielding faith in Allah. Despite possessing little material wealth, his heart was adorned with gratitude and contentment.

One day, Abdullah learned that the Prophet Muhammad, peace be upon him, was gathering the community for a special occasion. Eager and excited to be in the presence of the beloved Prophet, Abdullah made his way to the mosque, clad in his simple and well-worn attire.

As the gathering commenced, the Prophet welcomed each individual with a warm smile, ensuring that every person felt valued and equal in the eyes of Allah. Abdullah found his place among the congregation, enveloped in a sense of peace and belonging.

Observing Abdullah sitting quietly after the gathering, the Prophet, acknowledging the economic challenges he faced, approached him with kindness. "Abdullah, would you honor me with your presence for a meal at my home?" the Prophet asked.

Overwhelmed by the magnitude of such an invitation, Abdullah hesitated briefly but then graciously accepted. Together, they walked to the Prophet's modest dwelling, where the fragrance of unity and brotherhood permeated the air.

Seated for the meal, the Prophet treated Abdullah with the utmost respect and equality, serving him first and engaging in meaningful conversation. In that simple yet profound moment, Abdullah realized the depth of the Islamic principle that, regardless of worldly possessions, all believers are equal.

The companions, witnessing this poignant scene, were deeply moved by the Prophet's actions. They gleaned a profound lesson that day about the true essence of equality in Islam.

As Abdullah prepared to depart after the meal, the Prophet's words lingered in the air, "Abdullah, in the eyes of Allah, your worth is not determined by your wealth or status. It is your piety, humility, and kindness that truly matter."

This authentic story, found in various hadith collections, showcases the Prophet's unwavering commitment to building a society grounded in equality, justice, and compassion. The legacy of this encounter endured, echoing through generations and reminding all that, in Islam, every soul stands equal in the sight of Allah.

28. The Prophet and the Tribal Chiefs: Diplomacy and Tolerance

In the vibrant city of Mecca, during the formative years of Islam, a revered and wise leader, Prophet Muhammad, peace be upon him, carried the transformative message of peace and unity, inviting people to worship one God.

One decisive day, the Prophet set out to engage with the influential tribal chiefs of Mecca, recognizing the importance of gaining their understanding and support for the peaceful propagation of Islam. In the assembly of these powerful chiefs, the Prophet, accompanied by his close companion Abu Bakr, opted for a path of diplomacy and tolerance over confrontation.

With eloquence and respect, the Prophet addressed the gathering, explaining the fundamental principles of Islam and advocating for unity among the tribes. His words resonated differently with each chief—some listened intently, while others remained skeptical. Notably, Al-Walid ibn Al-Mughira, known for his opposition, tested the Prophet's patience.

In the face of skepticism and interruptions, the Prophet persisted in his peaceful dialogue. When asked to summarize the essence of Islam, he recited verses from the Quran, captivating the audience with the beauty and profundity of the message.

Despite facing resistance from those reluctant to relinquish tribal pride and influence, the Prophet adhered to his commitment to peaceful discourse. This event stands as a testament to his exemplary diplomatic skills and unwavering dedication to the principle of tolerance.

This encounter, marked by respectful conversation rather than forceful confrontation, laid the groundwork for future understanding. The seeds of dialogue planted during these diplomatic efforts would eventually blossom, as many tribal chiefs who initially opposed the Prophet embraced Islam. The wisdom and tolerance that defined the Prophet's approach became evident, offering a timeless lesson in diplomacy, patience, and the transformative power of peaceful dialogue in spreading the message of Islam.

29. The Cloak of Unity: Hadith al-Kisa

In the heart of Medina, the family of Prophet Muhammad, peace be upon him, exuded warmth and love. One day, a moment of concern arose as the Prophet's grandson, Hasan ibn Ali, fell ill. In response, the Prophet gathered his family, recognizing the healing power of unity.

In a simple yet profound gesture, the Prophet took his cloak, known as a "kisa," and spread it over Hasan, himself, Hasan's brother Husayn, their mother Fatimah, and their father Ali. Beneath the enveloping cloak, they formed a close-knit circle.

With hands raised in prayer, the Prophet sought Allah's mercy and blessings for his beloved family. This symbolic act conveyed the essence of unity, protection, and familial closeness.

The "Hadith al-Kisa," or the "Event of the Cloak," stands as a beacon highlighting the paramount importance of unity and the resilience that stems from a tightly woven family fabric. The Prophet's gesture underscored the idea that a united family, guided by love and faith, finds solace and strength amidst life's challenges.

This pivotal event served as a profound lesson for the broader Muslim community, emphasizing the significance of standing together, offering mutual support, and seeking blessings through the unifying bond of family. Documented in various Islamic sources, including both Sunni and Shia traditions, the "Hadith al-Kisa" continues to inspire Muslims globally, reinforcing the timeless principle that unity within the family is a wellspring of strength, resilience, and divine blessings.

30. The Farewell Pilgrimage: Prophet's Last Sermon of Divine Wisdom

In the vast expanse of the Arabian desert, bathed in the glow of the setting sun over Mecca, a multitude of believers gathered on the sacred plains of Arafat to witness a pivotal moment—the Farewell Pilgrimage, Prophet Muhammad's, peace be upon him, last journey of divine guidance.

Standing with humility on Mount Arafat, the Prophet addressed the diverse assembly, his noble countenance radiating a blend of solemnity and love. "O people, lend me an attentive ear," he began, recognizing the gravity of the moment. "For I know not whether, after this year, I shall ever be amongst you again in this place."

The attentive crowd fell into a hushed reverence, eagerly absorbing the profound words that followed.

"Your lives and your wealth are sacred and inviolable until you meet your Lord," he continued, establishing the sanctity of human life and property. "All mankind is from Adam and Eve; an Arab has no superiority over a non-Arab, nor a non-Arab over an Arab; a white has no superiority over a black, nor a black over a white, except by piety and good action."

These revolutionary words emphasized the foundational Islamic principle of equality among believers, irrespective of their backgrounds.

With a deep sense of responsibility, the Prophet dispensed divine guidance on various aspects of life. He stressed the importance of treating women with kindness and respect, reaffirming their rightful place in society. The Prophet also emphasized the paramount significance of justice as the bedrock of a righteous community.

Pointing his index finger skyward, the Prophet declared, "I leave behind me two things, and if you adhere to both of them, you will never go astray after me: the Book of Allah and my Sunnah (traditions)."

These words resonated through the hearts of the companions and reverberated across time, shaping the course of Islamic teachings.

As the sun gracefully descended below the horizon, marking the conclusion of the Farewell Pilgrimage, the Prophet, surrounded by a sea of believers, left them with a timeless sermon—a blueprint for a just and compassionate society. The wisdom shared on the plains of Arafat became a cherished legacy, guiding the believers through the ages and inspiring generations to come. The Farewell Pilgrimage stands as a testament to the Prophet's unwavering commitment to divine principles, fostering unity, justice, and piety within the Muslim community.

Years after the Farewell Pilgrimage, the words uttered on the plains of Arafat continued to echo in the hearts of the believers. The companions, now entrusted with the sacred task of preserving and disseminating the Prophet's teachings, carried forth the legacy of that momentous day.

The Farewell Pilgrimage had laid the groundwork for a just and compassionate society, and the companions embarked on the mission of implementing these principles in their daily lives. The egalitarian ethos, championed by the Prophet's sermon, began to shape the interactions within the Muslim community.

The wisdom encapsulated in the Prophet's farewell address served as a guiding light in times of triumph and tribulation. The Book of Allah, the Quran, became the enduring source of divine guidance, while the Sunnah—the Prophet's traditions and practices—provided a practical model for righteous living.

The companions, inspired by the Farewell Pilgrimage, worked tirelessly to establish a society that reflected the values enshrined in the Prophet's last sermon. They endeavored to uphold justice, respect the sanctity of life, and foster unity among the diverse believers.

As the Muslim community expanded and encountered new challenges, the timeless principles articulated on Mount Arafat provided a compass for navigating the complexities of life. The legacy of the Farewell Pilgrimage became a foundation upon which future generations would build their understanding of Islam.

The divine wisdom shared on that sacred occasion transcended the immediate context and addressed universal principles of morality, justice, and human relations. The Prophet's teachings on equality, justice, and adherence to divine guidance served as a beacon, guiding Muslims through the centuries.

The Farewell Pilgrimage, although a historical event, remained eternally relevant. Its impact rippled through the annals of Islamic history, influencing scholars, leaders, and communities. The principles articulated on that blessed day formed an integral part of the Islamic ethos, providing a moral compass for Muslims navigating the complexities of an ever-changing world.

In essence, the Farewell Pilgrimage was not merely a farewell; it was a legacy—a timeless gift bequeathed to humanity, encapsulating the essence of Islam and illuminating the path to a just, compassionate, and united society. The echoes of that sacred sermon resonated through the ages, reminding believers of their duty to embody the principles outlined on the plains of Arafat.

31. The Revelation of the Quran

In the serene solitude of the Cave of Hira, situated near Mecca, Prophet Muhammad, peace be upon him, sought moments of reflection and contemplation. It was the 27th night of Ramadan, in the year 610 CE, that the course of human history would be forever altered.

As the Prophet engaged in deep meditation, the silence was broken by the arrival of the Angel Gabriel, the celestial messenger of Allah. In a profound encounter that transcended the earthly realm, Angel Gabriel conveyed the first divine revelation to Prophet Muhammad, marking the initiation of the prophethood.

The words, powerful and eloquent, echoed through the cave, "Read in the name of your Lord who created, created man from a clot. Read, and your Lord is the Most Generous—Who taught by the pen—taught man that which he knew not" (Quran, 96:1-5).

Overwhelmed by the divine presence, Prophet Muhammad received the initial verses of what would later become the Quran—the holy scripture of Islam. This event, known as the first revelation, heralded the beginning of the prophetic mission and the conveyance of Allah's guidance to humanity.

The Prophet, initially bewildered by the magnitude of the divine revelation, sought solace in the unwavering support of his beloved wife Khadijah and the wise counsel of his close companion, Abu Bakr.

As subsequent revelations continued over the course of 23 years, the Quran addressed diverse aspects of human existence—guidance for personal conduct, laws for societal welfare, and reflections on the universe's creation. Each revelation was preserved meticulously by the Prophet's companions, ensuring the Quran's integrity.

The Revelation of the Quran stands as a testament to the divine wisdom and guidance that continues to inspire billions of Muslims worldwide. The transformative encounter in the Cave of Hira marked the inception of a message that transcends time and remains an eternal source of light and guidance for humanity.

32. The Hijra (Migration) to Medina: A Turning Point in Islamic History

In the year 622 CE, a crucial chapter in the life of Prophet Muhammad unfolded—the Hijra, or migration, from Mecca to Medina. This event, meticulously documented in authentic Islamic references, marked a transformative period in the history of Islam.

As Prophet Muhammad continued to convey the message of monotheism in Mecca, facing escalating opposition and persecution from the Quraysh tribe, the divine command for migration was revealed. The Prophet received guidance to seek refuge in Yathrib, a city north of Mecca, where a growing community awaited his arrival.

The Hijra was not a mere physical relocation; it symbolized a new era for the nascent Muslim community. In the darkness of the night, Prophet

Muhammad, accompanied by his closest companion Abu Bakr, stealthily left Mecca, narrowly escaping a Quraysh plot to assassinate him.

Upon reaching Quba, a suburb of Medina, the Prophet was warmly welcomed by the inhabitants. The spirit of brotherhood and unity among the Ansar (helpers) and the Muhajirun (migrants) laid the foundation for the establishment of the first Islamic state in Medina.

The Constitution of Medina, a landmark document drafted by Prophet Muhammad, served as a social contract, emphasizing religious tolerance and collaboration among the diverse communities in Medina. This historic pact created a cohesive society where Muslims and non-Muslims coexisted harmoniously.

The Hijra is so significant in Islam that it marks the beginning of the Islamic lunar calendar. This migration not only saved the Muslim community from persecution but also paved the way for the spread of Islam beyond the confines of Mecca. It exemplifies the importance of perseverance, trust in Allah, and the establishment of a just and inclusive society—an enduring lesson for generations to come.